Festivals

Day of the Dead

by Rebecca Pettiford

Bullfrog Books

Ideas for Parents and Teachers

Bullfrog Books let children practice reading informational text at the earliest reading levels. Repetition, familiar words, and photo labels support early readers.

Before Reading

- Discuss the cover photo. What does it tell them?

- Look at the picture glossary together. Read and discuss the words.

Read the Book

- "Walk" through the book and look at the photos. Let the child ask questions. Point out the photo labels.

- Read the book to the child, or have him or her read independently.

After Reading

- Prompt the child to think more. Ask: Have you ever celebrated Day of the Dead? What sorts of things do you see during this festival?

Bullfrog Books are published by Jump!
5357 Penn Avenue South
Minneapolis, MN 55419
www.jumplibrary.com

Library of Congress Cataloging-in-Publication Data

Names: Pettiford, Rebecca.
Title: Day of the dead / by Rebecca Pettiford.
Description: Minneapolis, MN: Jump!, [2017].
Series: Festivals | Includes index.
Identifiers: LCCN 2016022398 (print)
LCCN 2016026350 (ebook)
ISBN 9781620315316 (hard cover: alk. paper)
ISBN 9781620315859 (pbk: alk. paper)
ISBN 9781624964855 (e-book)
Subjects: LCSH: All Souls' Day—Juvenile literature.
Mexico—Social life and customs—Juvenile literature.
Classification: LCC GT4995.A4 P48 2017 (print)
LCC GT4995.A4 (ebook) | DDC 394.266—dc23
LC record available at https://lccn.loc.gov/2016022398

Editor: Kirsten Chang
Book Designer: Leah Sanders
Photo Researcher: Leah Sanders

Photo Credits: All photos by Shutterstock except: Alamy, 22; Getty, 3, 4, 5, 8–9, 14–15, 17, 20–21, 23bl, 24; Janmarie37/Shutterstock.com, 18–19; Kobby Dagan/Shutterstock.com, 16; Superstock, 6–7.

Printed in the United States of America at Corporate Graphics in North Mankato, Minnesota.

Table of Contents

Two Days with the Dead

It is November 1 in Mexico.

It is time for
Day of the Dead.

What happens?
We believe loved ones
who died come back.

They visit us as spirits.

It is not scary.

It is a happy time.

We visit Abuelo's grave.

Mama makes it pretty.

We remember him.

We tell stories
about his life.

We make an altar for him.
It has flowers.
It has sugar skulls.

sugar skull

10

It has pan de muerto.
Yum!

Look!

We put out a photo
of Abuelo.

We dress up.

We paint our faces.

Wow! Rosa looks
like a skeleton.

We go to a parade.

We see dancers.

17

There is music.

José plays a drum.

We dance.

We eat.

We celebrate life!

Day of the Dead Altar

food

candles

skeleton

flowers

Picture Glossary

Abuelo
The Spanish word for grandfather.

Mexico
A country south of the United States.

altar
A table used to honor and offer gifts to the dead.

pan de muerto
The name of this sweet bread means "bread of the dead" in Spanish.

grave
A place where a person is buried.

sugar skulls
Sugar shaped like human skulls are used as Day of the Dead decorations.

Index

To Learn More

Learning more is as easy as 1, 2, 3.

1) Go to www.factsurfer.com

2) Enter "DayoftheDead" into the search box.

3) Click the "Surf" button to see a list of websites.

With factsurfer.com, finding more information is just a click away.